NICK JONAS

SINGING SENSATION

KATIE LAJINESS

Big Buddy Books
An Imprint of Abdo Publishing
abdopublishing.com

BIG BUDDY **POP** BIOGRAPHIES

abdopublishing.com

Published by Abdo Publishing, a division of ABDO, PO Box 398166, Minneapolis, Minnesota 55439.
Copyright © 2016 by Abdo Consulting Group, Inc. International copyrights reserved in all countries.
No part of this book may be reproduced in any form without written permission from the publisher.
Big Buddy Books™ is a trademark and logo of Abdo Publishing.

Printed in the United States of America, North Mankato, Minnesota.
102015
012016

THIS BOOK CONTAINS
RECYCLED MATERIALS

Cover Photo: Associated Press.
Interior Photos: AF Archive/Alamy Stock Photo (p. 17); Associated Press (pp. 13, 23); Karen Bleier/
   AFP/Getty Images (p. 27); CBS Photo Archive/Getty Images (p. 17); Charley Gallay/Getty
   Images (p. 25); Scott Gries/Getty Images (p. 11); © iStockphoto.com (p. 9); © KMS/Splash
   News/Corbis (p. 19); Mathew Imaging/Getty Images (p. 15); Kevin Mazur/LP5/Getty Images
   (p. 29); © Walter McBride/Retna Ltd./Corbis (p. 6); Chris Pizzello/Invision/AP (p. 21); John
   Salangsang/Invision/AP Photo (p. 5).

Coordinating Series Editor: Tamara L. Britton
Contributing Editor: Marcia Zappa
Graphic Design: Jenny Christensen

Library of Congress Cataloging-in-Publication Data

Lajiness, Katie, author.
 Nick Jonas / Katie Lajiness.
    pages cm. -- (Big buddy pop biographies)
 Includes index.
 ISBN 978-1-68078-053-6
1. Jonas, Nick--Juvenile literature. 2. Singers--United States--Biography--Juvenile literature. I. Title.
 ML3930.J617L35 2016
 782.42164092--dc23
 [B]
                                    2015033043

CONTENTS

ROCK-STAR ACTOR

Nick Jonas is a talented singer, songwriter, and actor. He became known as part of the **pop** band Jonas Brothers. Today, Nick is a successful **solo** artist. Fans around the world love to see Nick **perform**!

SNAPSHOT

NAME:
Nicholas Jerry Jonas

BIRTHDAY:
September 16, 1992

BIRTHPLACE:
Dallas, Texas

SOLO ALBUM:
Nick Jonas

MAJOR APPEARANCES:
*Camp Rock, Jonas Brothers:
Living the Dream, Camp Rock 2,
Les Miserables, Hairspray,
Kingdom, Scream Queens*

FAMILY TIES

Nicholas Jerry Jonas was born in Dallas, Texas, on September 16, 1992. His parents are Denise and Paul Kevin Jonas Sr. His brothers are Kevin, Joe, and Frankie.

In 2010, Kevin, Denise, Joe, and Nick (*left to right*) went to an event at the White House.

WHERE IN THE WORLD?

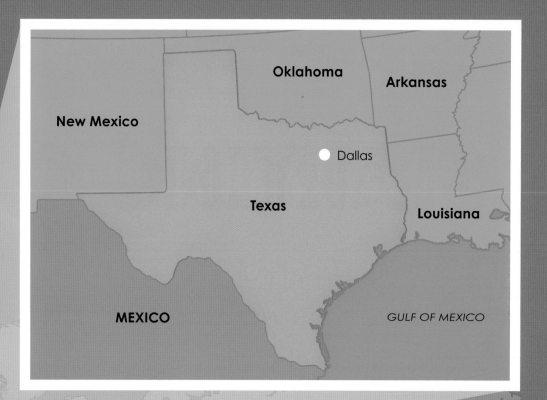

Oklahoma

Arkansas

New Mexico

● Dallas

Texas

Louisiana

MEXICO

GULF OF MEXICO

STARTING OUT

Growing up, Nick was a natural singer. By age seven, he was appearing in theater shows. Nick's first part was playing Tiny Tim in *A Christmas Carol*.

Nick liked **performing**. And, he wanted to be a singer. In 2002, Nick wrote his first song with his dad. It was called, "Joy to the World (A Christmas Prayer)." In 2004, he **released** his first album, *Nicholas Jonas*.

Nick performed on Broadway in New York City, New York. Broadway theater shows are famous for being some of the best in the world.

BIG BREAK

As kids, Nick, Kevin, and Joe enjoyed making music together. So, they decided to start a band. They called themselves the Jonas Brothers. In 2006, the band **released** its first album. *It's About Time* did not sell very well.

But by 2007, the band's music was played on Radio Disney and the Disney Channel. The Jonas Brothers became very popular with fans! The band put out new albums in 2007, 2008, and 2009.

Even though Nick (*center*) is younger than Kevin (*left*) and Joe (*right*), he was the band's leader.

The Jonas Brothers went on concert tours from 2005 to 2009. Starting in 2008, the Disney Channel made a show about Nick, Kevin, and Joe. It is called *Jonas Brothers: Living the Dream*. The show features the brothers backstage and on the road.

The band took a two-year break from 2010 to 2012. Each brother wanted to move his work in a new direction. So, the Jonas Brothers officially broke up in 2013.

In 2008, the Jonas Brothers performed in Times Square in New York City on New Year's Eve.

Nick and his brothers were known for their fun concerts. Nick even did flips on stage!

TALENTED ACTOR

In addition to singing, Nick is known for his acting abilities. He has starred in several large theater shows. Nick was in *Les Miserables* in London in 2010. In 2012, he had a **role** in the Broadway show *How to Succeed in Business Without Really Trying*.

In 2011, Nick appeared in *Hairspray* in Hollywood, California. He starred as Link Larkin.

Nick has also had acting **roles** in Hollywood, California. In 2008, the Jonas Brothers starred in *Camp Rock*. The band made *Camp Rock 2* in 2010. These were two of the Disney Channel's most-watched movies. In 2009, the brothers were voice actors in the movie *Night at the Museum: Battle of the Smithsonian*.

In 2014, Nick signed on to star in the television show *Kingdom*. He began to practice **mixed martial arts**. Nick built up his strength, so he could play the role of a fighter.

Nick, Kevin, and Joe voiced three cherubs in *Night at the Museum: Battle of the Smithsonian*.

From 2013 to 2015, Nick made guest appearances on the television show *Hawaii Five-O*. He plays a character who breaks into computer systems.

17

GOING SOLO

Nick was nervous about leaving the Jonas Brothers and singing his own music. But, he knew the kind of music he wanted to make as a **solo** artist. Nick put out his self-titled solo album in 2014. The album includes hit songs "Jealous" and "Chains."

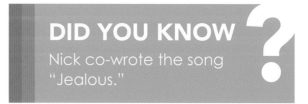

DID YOU KNOW?
Nick co-wrote the song "Jealous."

Because of his work with the Jonas Brothers, Nick already had many fans before his solo music came out.

Throughout 2014 and 2015, Nick **promoted** his new album. He **performed** on *The Ellen DeGeneres Show*, *The Voice*, and *Dancing with the Stars*. In September 2015, Nick started a 19-city **solo** tour. The album *Nick Jonas* reached number six on the Billboard 200 chart.

In 2015, Nick sang his song "Jealous" at the Billboard Music Awards.

AWARD SHOWS

Nick is no stranger to **award** shows. The Jonas Brothers won many awards. They include Nickelodeon Kids' Choice Awards, Teen Choice Awards, and an American Music Award.

In 2015, Nick **hosted** the Nickelodeon Kids' Choice Awards. The same year, he won the award for Favorite Male Singer!

DID YOU KNOW?

In 2015, Nick presented at the Tony Awards. These awards recognize excellence in live American theater.

Nick got slime dumped on him during the Nickelodeon Kids' Choice Awards!

OFF THE STAGE

When Nick has free time, he is involved with many benefits. Nick likes to help children. So, he has helped out the Make-A-Wish Foundation. This group grants the wishes of children with serious health conditions.

Nick also enjoys spending time with his family. They like to go **snowboarding** together.

Nick and Joe like to spend time together. In 2015, they attended a party for Nick's solo music.

A VOICE FOR DIABETES

Nick has **diabetes**. But, he doesn't let the condition get him down. Nick works hard to spread awareness about the illness.

Other people with diabetes look up to Nick as a **role model**. He spoke out for the American Diabetes Association. Nick also worked with Bayer Diabetes Care to help people with this condition.

Nick's diabetic fans like knowing that someone famous shares their illness.

BUZZ

Nick's fame continues to grow. In 2015, he was a guest **mentor** on the television show *The Voice*. And, he acted on the television show *Scream Queens*. Fans are excited to see what's next for him!

In 2015, Nick Jonas joined Taylor Swift on stage. They sang his hit song "Jealous."

GLOSSARY

award something that is given in recognition of good work or a good act.

diabetes (deye-uh-BEE-teez) a condition in which the body cannot properly take in normal amounts of sugar or starch.

host to serve as a host. A person who entertains guests.

mentor someone who teaches or gives help and advice to a less experienced person.

mixed martial arts a contact sport that allows a wide range of fighting techniques including striking, kicking, and grappling.

perform to do something in front of an audience.

pop relating to popular music.

promote to help something become known.

release to make available to the public.

role a part an actor plays.

role model a person who other people respect and try to act like.

snowboard to ride over snow in a surfing position on a board like a wide ski.

solo a performance by a single person.

WEBSITES

To learn more about Pop Biographies, visit **booklinks.abdopublishing.com**.
These links are routinely monitored and updated to provide
the most current information available.

INDEX

ATE DUE